Harry John Neville Vane,
11th Baron Barnard

Today, engendered by the confidence of centuries, that rare quality of peace and calm pervades, for the receptive visitor to savour.

Welcome to Raby Castle.

Contents

The Gatehouse

Overhead, as one passes through
the portcullis, are machicolations
through which boiling oil or
water could be poured on the
heads of attackers.

The stone figures originally
stood on the Barbican, now
demolished.

King Cnut

The first historic mention of Raby is early in the 11th century when the *Manor of Rabi* was one of the lands belonging to the township of Staindrop (then a provincial capital), which was gifted to the Prior of Durham by King Cnut, who reigned over England, Denmark and Norway from 1016 to 1035. It has long been thought that, at the time of the Conquest in 1066, Raby was in the possession of Sigurn, reputedly Cnut's niece.

Sir Henry Vane the Elder (1589 – 1654).

The Nevills were responsible for building the 14th century Castle which still stands today. They continued to live at Raby until 1569 when, after the failure of the *Rising of the North*, the Castle and its lands were forfeited to the Crown. In 1626, Sir Henry Vane the Elder, Member of Parliament and important member of Charles I's household (at first his Governor, later his Treasurer), purchased Raby from the Crown. His family still own Raby, the present owner being the 11th Lord Barnard.

Defended home

Although Raby is really a defended home rather than a fortress, it has seen action in battle, notably during the Civil War. Held by Sir George Vane for the Parliamentary forces, it was besieged in 1648 but suffered little damage. Although Sir Henry repaired Raby and carried out various building works, it was not until the 18th century that the first major alterations were made to the mediaeval structure. The 1st Lord Barnard, angered by his son's marriage, partly dismantled the Castle early in that century, but Henry, son of the 2nd Lord Barnard, later began a programme of restoration. Under the guidance of the architect James Paine, the interior of the South and West ranges underwent the greatest changes.

Henry, 1st Earl of Darlington (1705 – 1758).

Henry, 3rd Lord Barnard, was raised to the peerage as the 1st Earl of Darlington and it was his son, also Henry, 2nd Earl, who instigated the second period of renovation at Raby.

Henry, 2nd Earl of Darlington (1726 – 1792).

In 1768, he engaged John Carr to carry out improvements inside and outside the Castle, and on the Estate; the carriageway through the Entrance Hall was constructed at this time, and a round tower built on the South front to replace one burnt down earlier in the century. By the end of the 18th century, not only Raby Castle, but also its setting were considerably altered: the Moat was drained, the Park landscaped, the High and Low Ponds excavated, the Garden laid out and the Stables and ancillary buildings constructed.

William Harry
1st Duke of
Cleveland
(1766 - 1842).

The 3rd Earl, created Duke of Cleveland in 1833 for his political services, made no significant changes to the Castle, and it was not until his son Henry succeeded as 2nd Duke that the third major period of rebuilding began.

Top:
View of Raby Castle painted by
Joseph Miller of Staindrop (1844).

Middle and bottom:
Early 19th century views of Raby.

Henry,
2nd Duke of
Cleveland
(1788 - 1864).

In 1843 he invited William Burn to begin work on the Castle. Burn continued working at Raby over the next decade, in particular on the South front, his most notable achievement being the Octagon Drawing Room. The 9th Lord Barnard, after his accession in 1891, added touches to further enhance its architectural merit, but since then the Castle has remained little altered.

Tour of the Castle

Map of Raby Castle

S
E — W
N

Bulmer's Tower
Dining Room
Octagon Drawing Room
Library
Small Drawing Room

Joan's Tower

Entrance Hall

Servant's Bedroom

Blue Bedroom

Chapel Tower

Courtyard

Keep Tower

Nevill Gateway

← *Entrance*

Barons' Hall

Mount Raskelf

Watch Tower

Chapel

Kitchen Tower

Servants' Hall

Kitchen

Clifford's Tower

14th century *c.*1360 – 80

Late 14th century 1382 – 88

18th century & modern

Gatehouse

Entrance to Castle

Scale of feet

10 0 10 20   40   60   80   100

0   6   12   18   24   30

Scale of metres

and Park

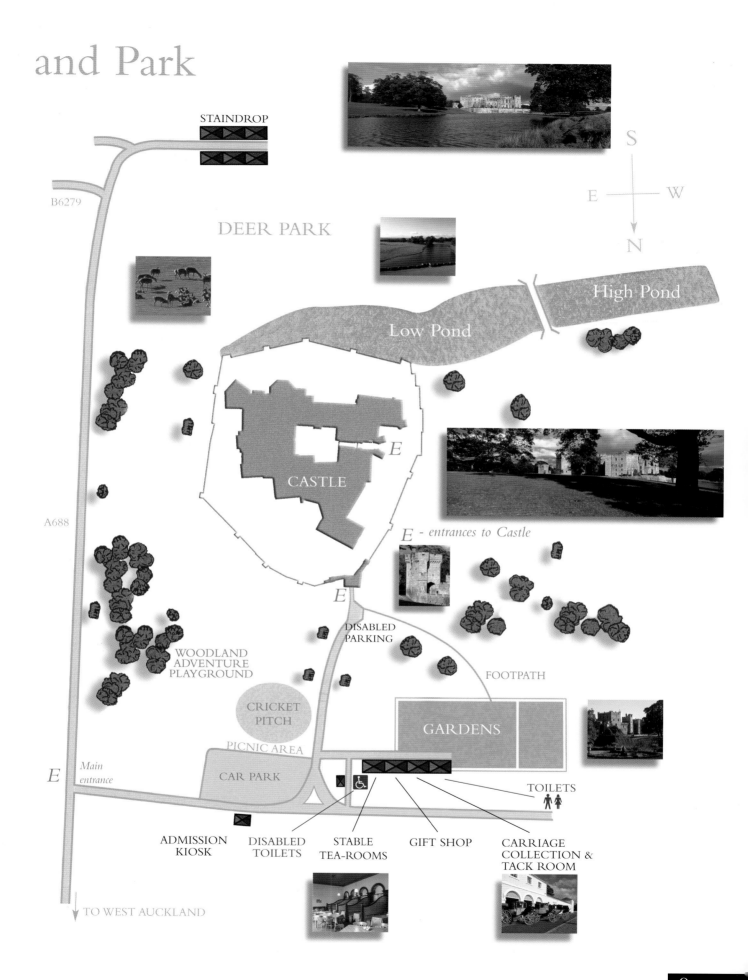

STAINDROP

DEER PARK

High Pond

Low Pond

CASTLE

E

E - entrances to Castle

E

DISABLED PARKING

FOOTPATH

E

WOODLAND ADVENTURE PLAYGROUND

CRICKET PITCH

PICNIC AREA

GARDENS

Main entrance

CAR PARK

TOILETS

ADMISSION KIOSK

DISABLED TOILETS

STABLE TEA-ROOMS

GIFT SHOP

CARRIAGE COLLECTION & TACK ROOM

TO WEST AUCKLAND

B6279

A688

S
E   W
N

Clifford's Tower

lies beyond the Gatehouse and at 24 metres high (79 feet), it is the largest in the Castle. It defended the Gatehouse and also rendered it untenable if captured. Its walls are immensely solid, being three metres thick even at the top. Some of the original Edward III windows remain, although Carr and Burn altered some, and inserted others. In the curtain wall joining this to the next tower, the Watchtower, 23 metres high (75 feet), more original windows remain. Behind the wall lies the mediaeval Guardroom of the Castle, now the Servants' Hall. Beyond the Watchtower is the great

Nevill Gateway, 19

metres high (62 feet), with its obliquely placed flanking towers, in mediaeval times the only entrance to the courtyard of the Castle. The Gateway itself, defended by the machicolations above, a portcullis and gate, of which traces may still be seen, has delicate lierne vaulting. Beyond lies a 21.5 metre-long barrel vaulted passage, again barred by a portcullis, and a door where marks made by a battering ram can still be seen today. Entrance to the Castle interior is through the Gateway and Courtyard. At the end of the tour,

when leaving the castle, the visitor can continue a tour of the exterior

by turning to the left.

Joan's Tower is 18

metres high (59 feet), and named after Joan Beaufort, 2nd wife of the 1st Earl of Westmorland. She was the daughter of John of Gaunt, half-sister to Henry IV and mother of the famous Cicely Nevill, Rose of Raby. The Terrace is overlooked by the South front, which owes its present appearance to Burn when he built the Octagon Drawing Room and extended the Barons' Hall above. Joined to the Octagon Drawing Room by the Dining Room, is the most unusual tower in Raby. **Bulmer's Tower**, is 23 metres high (75 feet), and named

after Bertram de Bulmer, grandfather of the Norman heiress, Isabella Nevill, whose marriage to the Saxon owner of Raby, Robert Fitzmaldred in the 12th century brought to Raby the illustrious name with which it was to be associated for over 300 years. Lord John Nevill heightened the tower and added the battlements in the 14th century, probably placing the Gothic 'b' upon two sides. Until the mid 18th century this unusual pentagonal tower was completely separate from the rest of the castle. It is unique in England, the only other tower

of this shape being in Denmark. An 18th century building by Carr joins this tower to the 22 metre

high (72 feet), ## Chapel Tower, which faces due East. Once the Barbican stood in front of this, onto which the guardrooms above the Chapel gave access. The Chancel window was inserted by Carr during his work to enable the new carriageway to pass through the Castle. Burn replaced the remaining windows although he copied the mediaeval traceries.

The next tower is ## Mount Raskelf, 21 metres high (69 feet), named after a Nevill manor in Yorkshire, joined to the Chapel tower by the now disused dairy built by Carr. The massive Kitchen Tower, containing the mediaeval Great Kitchen, built c.1370, is one of the finest in the country and adjoins Mount Raskelf. It is surmounted by a distinctive

octagonal lantern, raised in height to 23.5 metres (77 feet), by Carr. The windows were enlarged in the 19th century. A curtain wall joins this to Clifford's Tower, previously mentioned, where early leaded windows and arrow loops may be seen in the angle wall.

The East side of the Castle

showing from left;

Bulmer's Tower, Chapel Tower and Mount Raskelf   11

The Nevill Gateway, which leads to the
Courtyard and the Castle's entrance.

From the Courtyard, entrance to the Castle is through the mediaeval vaulted stone passage.

CHARLES NEVILL the SIXTH EARL of WESTMORLAND 1569

Charles Nevill 6th Earl of Westmorland

was the last of the Nevills to live at Raby Castle and the last Earl of Westmorland. He fled from here in 1569 after the *Rising of the North* and died in exile in Holland in 1601.

Mediaeval Passage & Lobby

The Mediaeval Passage leads to the Lobby, which is the work of James Paine, and Daniel Garrett, whose typical quatrefoil window may be seen on the West wall. The fireplace in the room is unusually placed directly underneath a window. Of particular interest in the Lobby is the portrait of the present owner of Raby, 11th Baron Barnard. The photograph of the 9th Lord Barnard in Masonic Regalia indicates the family's long involvement with the Craft.

Harry John Neville Vane, 11th Baron Barnard,

by Suzy Malin. 1985

Herbert Straker MFH, Master of the Zetland Hunt, by Sir Alfred Munnings P. R. A. Mr. Straker was the maternal Grandfather of the present Lord Barnard.

A pair of ponies harnessed for a carriage, with the initials (E.D.) Elizabeth Darlington, in the Stableyard at Raby, by J. F. Herring.

It is the fine collection of sporting pictures which gives the Small Drawing Room its special character, reflecting the family's strong interest in sporting pursuits of the 18th and 19th centuries. Here can be seen the work of most of the leading painters of sporting scenes, including Ben Marshall, J. F. Herring, H. B. Chalon, Francis Sartorius, John Wootton and Sir Alfred Munnings. The collection, one of the finest in the North of England, was probably begun by the 1st Duke of Cleveland and was added to by the 9th Lord Barnard.

Small Drawing Room

French ormolu clock, purchased at *The Paris Exhibition* in 1861.

Much of the architectural detail in this room dates from the 18th century when both Paine and Carr worked at Raby, however it was completely altered in 1820 to become a fine example of a Regency room. Facing south across the Park, the Small Drawing Room reflects in its atmosphere both the masculine sporting world of the Regency era, and the tranquillity of the landscape seen beyond the large windows.

The room retains its beautiful plaster ceiling which Perritt modelled for Paine, depicting musical instruments. From it hangs an English Regency chandelier of ormolu and crystal. The furniture includes many fine 18th and 19th century pieces, notably a walnut break-front bookcase which, dating from about 1710, is a very early example of its type, and a Regency giltwood side table in the manner of William Kent, on which stands an elaborate French clock of about 1860. Porcelain from the most famous manufacturers, including Bow figures, a Worcester vase, Davenport vases and Chelsea Derby cachepots may be seen around the room. There are also some attractive pieces of Regency glass.

In the short passageway through to the Library is a display case containing further examples of the family's collection of porcelain, including Worcester, Meissen and Derby pieces. Particularly worthy of note is a very fine gold painted Meissen bowl decorated by Herold, a noted painter of the Meissen factory *c.*1750.

Opposite:
Louise de Querouaille
'Madam Carwell',
Duchess of Portsmouth,
by Sir Peter Lely and Studio, formerly thought to be Nell Gwynne in a fine 17th century Sunderland carved giltwood frame. On either side are two large multi-tiered 18th century Chinese porcelain pagodas. Below the portrait is an 18th century George I black and gilt japanned coffer with chinoiserie decoration.

Library

Originally one long mediaeval room, the Library was divided into two rooms by Sir Henry Vane who engaged the noted architect Inigo Jones to work at Raby. James Paine removed the partition wall substituting Corinthian columns which remained until about 1870 when they were removed on the instructions of the 4th Duke of Cleveland. Formerly the Dining Room, it became the Library when Burn created the present Dining Room, and retained the name when it became a drawing room. The repetition of fox emblems on the pelmets, cornices and fireplace friezes reflects one of the favourite pursuits of the 1st Duke, whose arms decorate the gilded brass curtain restraints. The classical mouldings date from the time of Sir Henry Vane.

Dominating the room are two large ornamental Chinese pagodas of the Ch'ien Lung period and a Cantonese punch bowl of the same period stands on the William and Mary chest-on-stand. Between the two pilasters are 18th century gilt console tables in the style of William Kent. The walnut longcase clock is an early 18th century example by "Honest" George Graham, an eminent clock maker who was Master of the Company in 1722. The writing desk, with its inlaid panels of Sèvres porcelain is mid-19th century French, as are the twin chandeliers of ormolu and Paris porcelain.

18th century faience cockerel from the Nove factory.

Above the doorway is a portrait of *Sir Henry Vane the Elder*, and nearby the portrait of his son, *Sir Henry Vane the Younger*. Between them hangs the portrait of the *10th Lord Barnard*, and by the fireplace his wife, *Lady Barnard*, both by I. M. Cohen. Batoni's portrait of *William Bankes* is worthy of note as are the portraits of *Louise de Querouaille, Duchess of Portsmouth* and *Lady Mary Sackville* by Sir Peter Lely and Studio in their 17th century Sunderland frames.

Sir Henry Vane the Younger, circle of Gerard Soest.

Sir Henry Vane the Elder of Fairlawn, Kent and Raby Castle, by a follower of Michel Van Mierevelt.

Henry Vane, Earl of Darlington as an Oxford scholar, pencil and watercolour, by Richard Cosway R.A.

Ruins of a Classical temple,
by Marco and
Sebastiano Ricci.

Near the doorway to the
Ante-Library is an authentic-
looking key. It is in fact
made from papier-mâché,
and opens to form a fan.

Christopher William,
10th Baron Barnard
(1888 - 1964),
by I.M. Cohen.

Sylvia Mary,
wife of Christopher
10th Baron Barnard,
by I. M. Cohen.

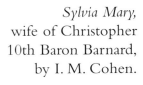

18

A detail of the 'Flemish' scarlet tortoiseshell and ebonised 17th century table cabinet-on-stand inlaid with floral marquetry.

The Ante-Library

The Ante-Library, an irregular-shaped room by Burn, adjoins the Library and contains an elaborate mid-17th century North Italian table cabinet, known as '*The Temple of Hymen*'. On the bookcase stands a miniature bureau, a Dutch apprentice piece of about 1720. The Victorian wallpaper is hand-blocked and gilded. The dummy board figure of 17th century style was a wedding present to the 10th Lord Barnard in 1920.

A Charles X ormolu clock by Thomire and Moinet Ainé of Paris. Modelled with Venus, Cupid and Cronos.

'An Artist's Studio', by David Teniers the Younger, *c.* 1640.

Octagon
Drawing Room
The restoration of a major Victorian interior.

The Octagon Drawing Room is a rare survivor of an 1840's room with unchanged decoration. Modelled in 1848 by the Scottish Architect William Burn from an existing circular room, the Octagon Drawing Room displays sumptuous textiles.

Gold silk lines the eight walls, and the curtains and elaborate swags are of crimson and gold silk. Sadly, by this century, the curtains had lost their swags, and sunlight had caused five of the panels and most of the curtains, to disintegrate.

The exterior of the Octagon Room - showing its shuttered windows - and above, the Barons' Hall.

A programme of works was undertaken in 1993 to renovate these textiles, which were described by the Victoria and Albert Museum as being astonishing, both in quality and quantity.

Where possible the silks were conserved by Caroline Rendell, but where this was impractical, new silks were woven by the Humphries Weaving Company on the only 19th century hand looms still in commercial use in England. When weaving was complete, the new panels, curtains and swags were manufactured and rehung by Albert Chapman of London, with silk trimmings to match the originals supplied by Wendy Cushing.

The paintwork and gilding was cleaned and conserved by the York firm of Hesp and Jones. Astonishingly, the ceiling required only to be washed, the original paint and gilding having survived in immaculate condition. Work to the mouldings surrounding the panels and to the carved and gilded pelmets was carried out by Whyttock and Reid of Edinburgh.

In the century and a half since the original design of the room, the suite of gilded furniture supplied for it by Morant of Bond Street had gradually been dispersed throughout the Castle, as fashions in furniture changed. However, using the 1864 inventory for identification, this has now all been collected together, restored where necessary and covered with the rich red and gold silk to match the curtains as it did originally.

The atmosphere of this historic room has been retained by sympathetic restoration and it has re-emerged as one of the most striking and instructive interiors of a decade that loved rich and colourful effects.

A Russian Alexander II malachite urn-shaped tazza standing on a giltwood side table of rococo design with malachite top.

HRH Frederick Prince of Wales (1707 - 1731), eldest son of George II by Amigoni, above a Victorian giltwood sidetable attributed to Gillow of Lancaster.

The Woodman by Thomas Barker of Bath.

Dining Room

This handsome Victorian room was also created by William Burn for Duke Henry. First designed as an oval room by Carr, the room was reconstructed by Burn to form a large formal dining room: the windows were extended into a bay, and an elaborate 'guilloche' design ceiling installed. The pattern of repetitive geometrically interlocking loops is a classical ornament, revived in Britain from the 16th to 20th centuries.

The furniture is mainly mahogany; the dining table by Gillow of Lancaster, is the style known as the Imperial, patented in 1806. The twin serving tables in the style of Thomas Hope, are of the Regency period, as are the wine cellarettes beneath them, one of them in the Egyptian style popular at that time. Beneath the marble-topped buffet table stands a plate bucket and a voiding bucket, for scraps. The barometer by the window is by Thomas Humphries of Barnard Castle, immortalised by Dickens in "*Master Humphries' Clock*".

Until 1962, when a nearby pantry was converted to provide a kitchen, all food had to be carried to the Dining Room from the Great Kitchen, 46 metres away. To keep food hot, dishes with hot water compartments and copper dish warmers were used. The installation of central heating *c.*1900 enabled a cast iron heated food cabinet to be placed in the corridor outside. As in many houses, the Dining Room also serves as a picture gallery. Among the many pictures here are the portraits of *Sir Henry Vane the Elder, No. 10,* by the Circle of Michel Van Mierevelt; *Sir Henry Vane the Younger, No. 17,* by Sir Peter Lely, and *Lady Katherine Powlett, No. 113,* cousin and 1st wife of the 3rd Earl of Darlington, by Sir Joshua Reynolds. Worthy of note is the double portrait, *No. 135,* by Cornelis De Vos of a *Gentleman and his wife.* The painting above the buffet table of *Marcus Curtius* by Luca Giordano, is one of three by this artist bought by the 2nd Duke of Cleveland and Southampton in 1749. Other interesting pictures are *The Woodman* by Thomas Barker of Bath, and the portrait by Jacopo Amigoni of *Frederick, Prince of Wales,* son of George II and father of George III, a friend of the 1st Earl of Darlington.

Lady Katherine Powlett by Sir Joshua Reynolds.

Entrance Hall

The impressive Entrance Hall, part of the original mediaeval structure of the Castle, was created in its present form by Carr for the 2nd Earl of Darlington to celebrate the coming of age of his heir in 1787. His imaginative scheme, with its graceful Gothic vaulting, described as "one of the boldest conceptions of its age and the first truly dramatic interior of the Gothic revival" was in part designed to ease the problems of turning carriages in the Courtyard. By constructing a tunnel under the Chapel and raising the roof of the Hall by

*The Entrance Hall c.*1800.
English School watercolour.

3 metres, he made it possible for carriages to drive right through the Hall. The carriageway can be traced in the difference in the paving of the floor. In the lifetime of the 10th Lord Barnard, when the Hunt met nearby, he and Lady Barnard and their family would have their horses brought to the Hall, and would ride from there to the Meet. Watercolour paintings show horses being ridden and led through the Hall.

A carved oak boar's mask
on a mid–Victorian bench.

The collection of arms and armour, and sporting trophies, reflects the military and sporting interests of many members of the family. The round of Brown Bess muskets, with their bayonets above, belonged to the South Durham Militia as did the sergeants' pikes nearby. Among the swords on the walls is that worn by the 2nd Earl at the Battle of Fontenoy. The armour and 'lobster pot' helmets are Cromwellian.

The furniture is mainly of oak, of particular interest being the Jacobean court cupboards in the Corridor. The leather-covered 'porter's chair' shielded its occupants from draughts, and has a cupboard underneath to hold a pot of glowing charcoals. In the 19th century, a band would play in the Entrance Hall during dinner and for the dancing which followed. The white marble statues of female figures at the lower end of the Hall are in the manner of J. M. Rysbrack depicting '*Painting*' and '*Architecture*'. Other statues are the bronze replicas of the *Venus de Medici* and the *Dying Gladiator*, in the Corridor. The bronze pendant lamps in the Corridor were originally designed for use with colza oil.

The graceful marble statue of the '*Greek Slave*', praised by Elizabeth Barrett Browning, is by Hiram Powers, an American sculptor. It caused a sensation when he exhibited it at the Great Exhibition of 1851 and was purchased by Duke Henry in 1861.

27

Servant's Bedroom

In contrast to the crowded Victorian bedroom of a member of the family, the Servant's Bedroom, reconstructed as it might have been in about 1900, is much more starkly furnished. That there are any ornaments at all, shows that this was the bedroom of a superior servant, in this case the Head Housekeeper. Only such servants had rooms to themselves, others sharing two or three to a room, although each had a separate bed. The furnishings include other items provided for senior servants, such as the wardrobe, others making do with pegs or a cupboard built into the wall, and an armchair. The carpet would have once graced a more important room, but it was an improvement on linoleum.

Blue Bedroom

This bedroom is one of the rooms created by John Carr in the late 18th century, although Burn altered it in about 1845 when he constructed the Bulmer's Tower staircase nearby. Not all of the contents are original, but have been brought from other rooms in the Castle to show how a typical bedroom in Raby might have looked at this period. The large State bed, of a type known as a Polonaise because of its domed canopy surmounted by a coronet, is of deal, grained to resemble pollard oak, and the coat of arms of the Earl of Darlington and his second wife, Elizabeth Russell indicates a date of about 1815. The Marseilles quilting of the bedcover depicts the Royal Coat of Arms of the Prince Regent, later King George IV, who visited Raby in 1806.

The remaining furniture is mainly 19th century and English, although the dressing cheval mirror and two small armchairs are French. The toilet table, which like the dressing table displays the cypher of Duke Henry, is equipped with a fine Victorian washing table set of about 1860. The ornate looking glass on the dressing table is Venetian, late 18th or early 19th century. Behind the screen, covered in hand-painted 18th century Chinese wallpaper is a hip bath and mahogany bidet, which would have been filled with jugs of hot water carried upstairs by servants. Note the bellpushes on either side of the fireplace, used for summoning servants.

Paintings of particular note are, by the door, *Portrait of a Lady, No. 93,* by John Michael Wright, the favoured painter of the Cromwellian faction; above the wardrobe, a portrait of *The Empress Marie Louise, No. 121,* second wife of the Emperor Napoleon, by Lefèvre; and on the window wall *Music Hath Charms, No. 162,* a cottage interior with a blind fiddler and children by Alexander Hohenlohe Burr.

The room has recently been redecorated, using a reproduction 19th century wallpaper, while the new Brussels-weave carpet has been copied from the original supplied for this room in 1848 by a local carpet manufacturer.

Barons' Hall

Little now remains of the original mediaeval structure of the Hall, which once held seven hundred knights, all feudal retainers of the Nevills, where *The Rising of the North* was plotted in 1569.

During the construction of the carriageway, Carr had raised the floor level by 3 metres; he also replaced some of the decaying 14th century window traceries, but retained the existing hammerbeam roof. Burn extended the room by 17 metres over his Octagon Drawing Room and replaced the roof with the present more elaborate one. The pointed Gothic embrasures assumed a rounded, more Norman appearance, while those on the East side were walled in, two only remaining as recesses. Only those windows on the West side and that above the Minstrels' Gallery remain from the Nevill period. The traceries of the South bay window, in which are inserted stained glass armorial panels, executed by Willement for the 4th Duke of Cleveland, Duke Harry, are copied from the originals, removed when the extension was built. The 600 year old stone Minstrels' Gallery was considerably changed to allow the insertion of the doorway to the Grand Staircase beyond in 1864.

The large Meissen birds which surmount the fireplaces are by Kandler and Kirchner and were made for the Japanese Palace in Dresden about 1730. Other porcelain in the room is mainly Oriental.

Because of the action of the 1st Lord Barnard, none of the original furnishings remain, and the earliest pieces are the Jacobean court cupboards and the Queen Anne gaming tables with their Beauvais tapestry tops. Most of the furniture is Georgian or Victorian. Of particular interest are the High Gothic tables in Zebra wood, with the associated suite, whose design has been attributed to Pugin, and the rose and gilt suite by Gillow. Two chairs from the Coronation of Her Majesty the Queen are the

most modern pieces of furniture in the Hall alongside chairs from the Coronations of George VI and Edward VII. At the South end, on the floor, is the Raby Tapestry, a carpet worked by Lady Grace Fitzroy, wife of the 1st Earl of Darlington and grand-daughter of Charles II and Barbara Villiers. Her portrait hangs beside the door.

The portraits in the Barons' Hall are of the family and their connections. *The 1st Lord Barnard, No. 31*, and his wife, *Elizabeth, No. 33*, whose anger at the marriage of their son *Gilbert, No. 39*, to *Mary Randyll, No. 40*, has already been mentioned, should be noted, as should *Capt. the Hon. Raby Vane in the uniform of the Honourable East India Company Marine* by Sir Joshua Reynolds, *No. 105*, and the full-

length portrait of *Elizabeth, 1st Duchess of Cleveland*, by Hoppner, *No. 114*. There is a watercolour painting of the Hall during Burn's alterations, showing its use as a grand saloon.

Meissen eagle: one of five superb pieces in the Hall, made by Kandler & Kirchner, for the Japanese Palace in Dresden, between 1727-1732.

Barons' Hall

Although Carr designed a staircase from the Barons' Hall to the Entrance Hall, it was not completed until 1864, to a design by Austin and Johnson of Newcastle. The heraldic beasts on the pillars of the landing are the supports of Duke Harry's arms, which they bear on escutcheons.

Important pictures hang on the staircase, notably *The Circumcision of Christ*, and *The Adoration of the Magi*, by Luca Giordano, and *A Group of Musicians*, by the Venetian School, early 18th century after Paolo Veronese. On either side of the staircase are 18th century Dutch figures of a Serving Girl and a Goose Boy.

Chapel

The mediaeval Chapel, which has been dated between 1364 and 1367, was once completely separate from the rest of the Castle, and until Duke Henry's restoration in 1848, had long been neglected. The floor, which had been raised three metres by Carr during the construction of the carriageway below, was lowered one metre by Burn. At the same time he replaced the original decayed window traceries, and open couple roof with replicas. The stone walls were stoothed and the six light arcade plastered over.

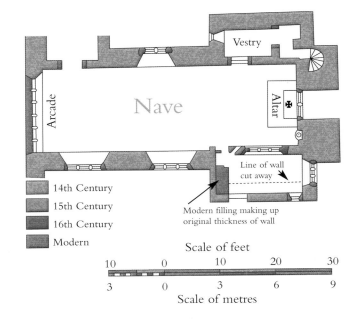

Vestry

Arcade

Nave

Altar

Line of wall cut away

Modern filling making up original thickness of wall

14th Century
15th Century
16th Century
Modern

Scale of feet

| 10 | 0 | 10 | 20 | 30 |

| 3 | 0 | 3 | 6 | 9 |

Scale of metres

As part of his further restoration in 1901, the 9th Lord Barnard uncovered the arcade and commissioned portraits of people associated with Raby during the Nevill period, whose likenesses are taken from tomb effigies and stained glass windows. On the extreme right of the arcade is the painting of Cicely, Rose of Raby, mother of Edward IV and Richard III, grandmother of Edward V and Elizabeth Plantaganet, wife of Henry VII and thereby an ancestress of our present Royal family.

13th century stained glass depiction of a monk, thought to be from the School of Caen, in France.

12th century stained glass from the Abbey of St. Denis, near Paris, depicting St. Benedict awaiting the arrival of his servant Romanus, to feed him.

The present High Gothic decor of the Chapel and the carved oak pew ends date from 1901 as well as the stained glass window above the altar, which bears the arms of the 9th Lord Barnard recording his marriage to Lady Catherine Cecil, 3rd daughter of the 3rd Marquess of Exeter. The remaining windows were redesigned at this time, as well as 19th century armorial glass designed for Duke Harry, panels of ancient stained glass were inserted. In the second South window, two panels from the 12th century Abbey of St. Denis showing the *Dream of the Magi*, and *St. Benedict in his cave* may be seen in the upper traceries. Below these are two fine English roundels which originally graced the Abbey at Whitby.

The paintings are mainly Italian. Near the Altar hang *The Descent from the Cross* after Daniele da Volterra, *The Madonna in Prayer* by the Circle of Carlo Dolci, and *Ecce Homo* by Guido Reni. Above the door is *Christ holding the Cross* attributed to the Spanish School, 17th century, next to *The Holy Family*, after Raphael. A large watercolour, *The Sermon on the Mount*, hangs above the arcade.

Lord Barnard's second eldest daughter, Elizabeth, was married here in January 1982 and the font was restored in 1990 and has since been used for several family Christenings.

An heraldic supporter of the family coat of arms on a pew end.

35

The ceiling vault, with its four intersecting arches, sweeps upward to meet an octagonal ventilation shaft which provides a strong updraught to remove smoke and fumes. This lantern was increased to its present height of 21 metres by Carr.

Kitchen

The Kitchen is one of the most remarkable rooms at Raby, for it retains almost completely its original mediaeval form. It was built in 1360, and was in use for the next six hundred years until 1954. Although the windows were enlarged in the 17th century and again subsequently and improvements made in the cooking equipment, the basic structure was retained.

The Kitchen boasts a vast array of copperware, including moulds of all descriptions, kettles, pans and steamers as displayed on the dressers.

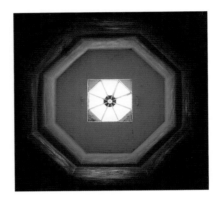

Across the corners run massive strengthening beams; sides of meat and hams could be hung from them by means of ropes fastened to pegs still visible on the walls.

The reflective surfaces provided by the stepped and vaulted window recesses increased available light. Around the room runs a passageway set within the thickness of the walls, which was used both as a defensive position by soldiers guarding the Castle and as a serving passageway to the Barons' Hall.

Cooking would originally have been done on open fires using cauldrons and spits turned by scullions or dogs. Later the fireplaces were filled in with the present iron ranges, one of which has a spit turned by the convection of hot air. Beside the door is a bread oven. The sinks nearby were used for heating water by means of a fire lit beneath them.

One of the tables has a marble inset for pastry making, although there was a separate room, now demolished, especially for this purpose. Vegetable preparation and the scouring of pots and pans took place in the sculleries, erected in the mid–18th century, next door.
On the floor of the second scullery are mediaeval terracotta floor tiles, probably removed from the Entrance Hall during Carr's alterations.

Servants' Hall

The Servants' Hall is another of the surviving mediaeval parts of the Castle. The windows facing onto the Courtyard are original, but those facing outwards were once arrow-loops and have been enlarged. This room is thought to have been the Guardroom. During the Civil Wars it was the main garrison, where weapons, horses and men could be placed in relative safety.

Minton plates on display in dresser.

Although the Hall may seem cold and austere now, in the days when it was in full use it would have been a warm and jolly place, with a fire always burning in the hearth, and the staff relaxing or carrying out tasks such as knife polishing and sharpening.

Lunch was the only meal eaten in the Hall by all servants. After the first course, the Butler, Housekeeper and Lady's Maid would retire to the Housekeeper's Room to finish their meal. The Cook never joined the other servants but was served in the Cook's Sitting Room next to the Kitchen. At lunch, beer would be drunk, served in the large jugs seen in the Hall. The mahogany trays enabled bread to be passed easily from one end of the table to the other.

The dresser at the end contains
Minton plates painted with a design
of feathers, no two being the same.
There are also Doulton ware cider or
beer jugs, together with little
earthenware and copper moulds,
some of which display the "C" for
the Dukes of Cleveland.

At this point, the tour of the Castle
moves into the Courtyard and then
through the Nevill Gateway. Of
note on the way is the sundial on the
Keep, and the small barred window
on its top storey, behind which is the
room traditionally occupied by
Cicely Nevill, the Rose of Raby.

The Park

Raby Park, which extends to 101 hectares (250 acres), is now part of Raby Home Farm. When Raby was first built (over 600 years ago), there were three deer parks, all heavily wooded and providing game for the owners. Gradually this woodland was cleared and the land cultivated until, in the mid-18th century, the 2nd Lord Barnard, influenced by the prevailing fashion for landscaping, commissioned Thomas White to work at Raby. By 1748 the Ponds had been constructed, while the Moat was drained later in the century. The Gazebo, to the North of High Pond, was designed by Daniel Garrett. Apart from extending the Ladywood at the South end of the Park, and the planting of the North Wood, little work took place during the 19th century, and it was not until the 20th century that further planting took place. The 10th Lord Barnard, was a keen forester, and took great interest in the Park, establishing further clumps and plantations. The small clump at the corner of Low Pond was planted to celebrate the Silver Jubilee of King George V in 1935.

An avenue of limes has been planted near the Car Park to replace elms removed through Dutch elm disease. Over 30 types of trees may be seen in the Park with beech being the most numerous. On the Terrace, North of High Pond, the avenue of fine mature beech trees has been partially felled and replanted, a high fence protecting the young trees from the predations of the deer and other animals.

A herd of Longhorn Cattle graze alongside the deer in the Park, which also provides the habitat for many birds, some of which are found all year round while others are seasonal.

The East side of the Castle, seen beyond one of the Park's splendid oaks.

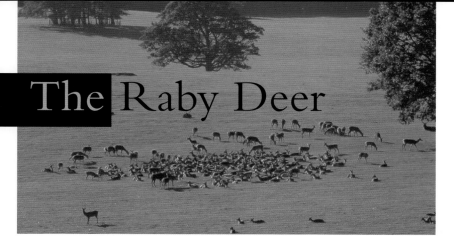

The Raby Deer

Two kinds of deer, Red and Fallow including a few White Fallow are to be found in Raby Park. The Red deer is much larger than the Fallow, and is the largest British wild land mammal. Both herds contain the descendants of deer preserved in this area since Norman times. During the Summer months the males and females separate, coming together for the mating season, or rut, which for Red deer, starts about the middle of September, with the Fallow deer mating from the middle of October.

The male of the Red deer is known as a stag, and the female a hind. Their young are born in May or June, usually near the birth place of the mother. All newly born deer are spotted, but after six weeks they lose this baby coat and grow a brown one. Males start to grow antlers the Spring after they are born. These increase in size each year until at four years old a stag is an eight pointer, that is each antler has four prongs or points. During March and April they shed their antlers and start new growth. Until this is complete, it is covered with red brown hair, and at that time the stag is said to be "in velvet". The main food of the Red deer is grass and foliage. This is augmented during the Winter with hay, clover and mangolds. Young trees need to be protected from browsing deer, and fallen branches will be quickly stripped of leaves.

Generally, Fallow deer are smaller than Red deer but those bred in parks such as Raby are larger than wild ones. There are at least three types of Fallow deer: dark grey, known as Black Fallow, the type mainly found at Raby; mottled with white spots; and plain white, also found in Raby Park. White deer are always park bred, while the dark grey are in general originally from the wild. The male of the Fallow is known as a buck, while the female is a doe. The young, born in June and July, are known as fawns and are also spotted. The development of the Fallow buck is similar to that of the Red stag but the mature antlers are clubbed rather than pointed. Fallow deer eat grass, young shoots, forest fruits, chestnuts and acorns, and during Winter their diet is also supplemented.

Gardens

Although there would have been a small garden at Raby during the Middle Ages to provide the herbs and plants needed for medicines, and those few fruits and vegetables which were available, it was not until the mid-18th century that a formal garden was established, designed by Thomas White.

The sloping, South-facing Walled Garden, bounded on two sides by a ha-ha, currently extends to five acres, although as first laid out, it was much larger. The walls of locally hand-made bricks were constructed with flues which, when heated, enabled sub-tropical fruits such as apricots to be grown on the South Terrace. Of these, only the White Ischia fig brought to Raby in 1786 by William Harry, Lord Barnard, later 3rd Earl of Darlington, still survives in its specially built house, fruiting annually. In the 19th century, the Raby Castle red currant (*Rubus rubrum*) was developed by the then Head Gardener, and may still be seen in the West Garden.

The Gardens have been considerably altered during this century, particularly since 1980, but many of the original features remain, in particular the two fine old yew hedges, and the ornamental pond, originally constructed to provide water for the Kitchen Garden, which dominates the Central Garden. Also within this area are the new

Conservatory, whose front replicates the 19th century original, the rose gardens, formal lawns and the informal heather and conifer gardens.

The East Garden contains the main herbaceous border, designed by the wife of the 10th Lord Barnard, with species of trees within the lawn, such as the tulip tree (*Liriodendron tulipifera*) and the Wedding Day Rose (*Rosa syn 'Wedding Day'*), whose petals transform through three colour changes.

The West Garden displays shrub borders, garden nurseries and the remaining Kitchen Garden. Also in this part of the Garden is the Gothic Cottage orné designed by James Paine.

In the centre of the South Terrace is a fine wrought iron gate, bearing the monogram of Christopher, the 1st Lord Barnard. Designed by James Gibb it was made originally in the early 18th century for Shipbourne Church, near the family seat of Fairlawn in Kent, and when the Church underwent repairs in the late 19th century, the then owner of Fairlawn, Mr Cazalet, made a gift of it to the 9th Lord Barnard, who erected them here in 1894. A smaller gate in the wall of the East Garden was erected by the wife of the 10th Lord Barnard in 1937.

In the Coach Yard, to be found opposite the Car Park, are the Coach Houses and entrance to the Gardens. These stand on the site of the original main road from Staindrop to Cockfield with houses of the old mediaeval village of Raby on either side, of which only Byre House at the entrance of the Coach Yard now remains, gothicised by Carr.

Coachyard & Carriage Collection

The Coach Houses were designed by Carr in about 1775 and house fine examples of the coachbuilders' craft, including two late 18th century travelling chariots, bearing the arms of the Earl of Darlington, which would have been drawn by a pair of horses – usually matched Cleveland Bays; the Raby State Coach, built in the early 19th century for the Duke of Cleveland, last used in 1902 for the Coronation of Edward VII, by the 9th Lord Barnard, whose arms appear on the side panels; a Governess cart, designed for the safe transport of children; a caned whisky, which, with its light body easily drawn by a Shetland pony, was used for pleasure excursions in the Park and local neighbourhood; and a station cart and estate cart, both dating from the 19th century. Also on view are hand-operated horse-drawn fire engines, with their leather water buckets, which were manned by estate employees. In the Tack Room the harnesses and other trappings for the coach horses, together with a more exotic Arab saddle cloth and harness are displayed. Livery worn by the Coachman in the Edwardian period may also be seen.

The Stables for the coach horses have been turned into Tearooms for visitors; the original stalls have been retained, some of them bearing the names of their former occupants.

The State Coach in black
and yellow livery, built by
Rigby & Robinson of Park
Lane, London, for the Duke of
Cleveland c.1810 – 1820, showing
the coat of arms of the 9th Lord
Barnard. It was last used for the
Coronation of Edward VII in 1902.

The Lords of Raby

Although the first mention of Raby (then spelled Rabi) was in the reign of **Cnut**, when he ruled Denmark, Norway and England, styling himself *Emperor of the North*, apart from his offering the Manor of Rabi to the Church, there is no evidence that he occupied the manor house which stood on the site before the Castle was built.

In 1131 the Manor of Raby was granted to **Dolfin, son of Uchtred** (and descendant of Malcolm II, King of Scots), by the Prior of Durham. This Dolfin married Adelicia, niece of Bishop Flambard, who built Durham Cathedral; their son, Maldred was the father of Robert Fitzmaldred who married Isabella Nevill, a great Norman heiress, who eventually inherited the Manors of Sheriff Hutton near York and Brancepeth, together with lesser lands and manors. Their son, **Geoffrey Nevill**, taking his mother's name, was the first Nevill owner of Raby, and it continued in the possession of this family, at one time the most powerful in England, until 1569.

The next owner of Raby, **Robert Nevill**, d. 1282, was Castellan, during Henry II's war with the Barons, of Bamburgh, Scarborough and Newcastle. He was succeeded by his grandson, **Ranulf, 1st Baron Nevill**, whose father, Robert, had married Mary, daughter of Robert FitzRanulf. This Ranulf, who died in 1331, was in turn succeeded by his second son, **Ralph**, whose brother Robert Nevill, known as *The Peacock of the North*, was slain at Berwick in 1319 by the Black Douglas. Ralph, 2nd Baron Nevill, was also captured by the Black Douglas in the same fray, but was ransomed and fought in further campaigns against the Scots, and was the victor of the Battle of Nevill's Cross at which he took prisoner David II, King of Scotland. He was a great benefactor of the Church, and when he died in 1367, was the first layman to be buried in Durham Cathedral.

He was succeeded by his eldest son, **John, 3rd Baron Nevill, KG**, who completed the building of the present castle, having obtained a licence to crenellate in 1378, although this probably meant adding fortifications to an existing building. He was a great captain, being appointed Governor of Aquitaine, 1378-81, Lord Warden of the Marches, and Joint Commissioner for treating for peace with Scotland. He died in 1388 and was buried in the Nevill Chantry in Durham Cathedral, where his tomb was much mutilated by Scottish prisoners during the Civil War.

John, Lord Nevill, was succeeded by his son, **Ralph**, mentioned by Shakespeare in Henry V, who was created Earl of Westmorland in 1397, the first to hold this title, by Richard II, but he afterwards joined the Lancastrians and was instrumental in placing his brother-in-law, Henry IV, on the throne. In return, the King created him Earl of Richmond, a Knight of the Garter and Earl Marshal of England. His first wife was Lady Margaret Stafford, by whom he had seven children, and his second Lady Joan Beaufort, daughter of John of Gaunt, by whom he had a further fourteen children. Their youngest daughter, Cicely, the Rose of Raby, married Richard, Duke of York, and was the mother of Edward IV and Richard III. Through her grand-daughter Elizabeth, Queen of Henry VII, she is an ancestress of the Royal family. The Earl's youngest son, Edward, was created Baron Bergavenny and his descendant, the Marquess of Abergavenny, is the present head of the Nevill family. The Earl was a great church builder, and his alabaster tomb in Staindrop Church, where his effigy lies between that of his two wives, is regarded as being among the finest monuments in the North. He died in 1425.

His successor, his grandson, **Ralph 2nd Earl of Westmorland**, who died in 1484, engaged in inconclusive private warfare with his uncles of the Earl's second marriage over the Middleham Estates, which had been left to them through the influence of their mother, until both sides were commanded by Henry VI to keep the peace. He was succeeded by his nephew, **Ralph, 3rd Earl**, whose father was killed fighting for the Red Rose (Lancastrians) at the Battle of Towton, 1461. The 3rd Earl, who fought in Scotland against Perkin Warbeck, died in 1523, and again was succeeded by a grandson, also **Ralph, 4th Earl** another energetic warrior against the Scots. He was present at the Field of the Cloth of

Gold, and was a signatory to the letter of Pope Clement asking for the divorce of Queen Catherine of Aragon.

Before his death in 1549, the Earl was created a Knight of the Garter. He was succeeded by his son **Henry, 5th Earl**, who as a boy took part in the Pilgrimage of Grace. He was a staunch supporter of Queen Mary Tudor and under her,

held High Office. The family adhered firmly to the Old Faith, and his son **Charles Nevill, 6th and last Earl of Westmorland**, was leader, with Thomas Percy, of the ill-fated rebellion, *The Rising of the North*, in support of Mary Queen of Scots, in 1569.

He fled to Holland where he died in 1601. Thus ended the Nevill ownership of Raby, which had lasted for nearly 400 years. The Castle was held by the Crown until 1626 when it was purchased by **Sir Henry Vane the Elder**.

THE VANES

According to various Visitations of Kent, the Vanes are descended from **Howell ap Vane** or Fane of Monmouthshire, but had settled in Kent by 1426. Henry Vane, in accordance with the rules of chivalry, whereby one knight could surrender only to another, was knighted by the Black Prince at the Battle of Poitiers in 1356, after he had accepted the surrender of the French king who, in submission, offered his golden gauntlet, which has ever since been a charge on the Vane coat-of-arms.

Sir Henry Vane the Elder, who purchased Raby in 1626, was the son of Sir Henry Vane, of Hadlow, Kent. Born in 1589, he was a distinguished statesman under both James I and Charles I, and an important politician, being appointed a Member of the Privy Council in 1630. In 1640, he was appointed Secretary of State, a post he held only until 1641, when he fell from favour after the attainder of Strafford, in which he was instrumental. At this time, he joined the Parliamentary party. When Civil War broke out, he was appointed Lord Lieutenant of Durham, a strongly Royalist county where he had no real authority. After the death of the King in 1649, to which he was opposed, he continued to sit in Parliament, but because of opposition to Cromwell's policies, ceased to take an active part. Sir Henry

died in Kent in 1654, where he was buried in Shipbourne Church near the family seat of Fairlawn and was succeeded by his eldest son, Henry, known as **Sir Henry Vane the Younger**.

Born in 1613, Sir Henry studied at the University of Oxford and later, having been converted to Puritanism, at Leyden and Geneva. In 1635, he went to Massachusetts where, because of his high connections, and despite his youth, he was elected Governor of the Colony for 1636-7. Although his period as Governor was not wholly successful, he retained an interest in the American Colonies after his return to England and later used his influence to help them develop. Elected to Parliament in 1639, he was one of the leaders of the War party at the commencement of the Civil War, but in 1646 his leadership of this party ended, and when the dispute between the Army and Parliament started in 1647, Sir Henry generally absented himself from Parliament. He took no part in the trial of the King, nor consented to, nor approved of his execution. After the death of the King, Sir Henry was appointed to the Governing Council but, becoming increasingly opposed to the policies of the Protector, retired from Parliament in 1653. Refusing to accept Cromwell as Head of State as well as the Army, he was imprisoned on the Isle of Wight for some time in 1656, but after the death of Cromwell returned to Parliament and acted as mediator between the Army and the House. At the restoration in 1660, he was again imprisoned, in the Tower and then on the Scilly Isles, his republican principles being regarded as seditious. In 1662, despite a promise given by Charles II to Parliament at the time of the Restoration that he would be spared, Sir Henry was executed. Pepys recording that he died 'with all humility and gravity'.

He was succeeded at Raby by his second son, **Thomas**, the eldest son Henry having died in 1660. Thomas Vane was elected M.P. for the County of Durham in 1675, but died shortly afterwards, and was succeeded by Sir Henry's fifth son,

Christopher. He was made a Privy Councillor by James II, but later supported William and Mary, by whom he was raised to the Peerage in 1698 as the **1st Baron Barnard**.

Although at this time Fairlawn was the family's principal seat, Raby was entailed on Lord Barnard's heir Gilbert, and disapproving of their son's marriage, Lord Barnard and his wife  Elizabeth tried to disinherit him by starting to pull down the Castle, but were ordered to desist by the Courts and forced to make restitution. In 1723, Lord Barnard died, and was succeeded by **Gilbert, 2nd Baron Barnard**, under whom a programme of restoration of the Castle and landscaping of the Park started. He died in 1753 and was succeeded by his eldest son **Henry, 3rd Baron**  **Barnard**, who was created the **Earl of Darlington** in 1754. The Earl, a keen politician and friend of Frederick Prince of Wales, married Lady Grace Fitzroy, granddaughter of Charles II and Barbara Villiers, who had been created Duchess of Cleveland and Southampton in her own right. In 1758 the Earl died, and was succeeded by his eldest son, **Henry, 2nd Earl of Darlington**.

The 2nd Earl, a soldier and politician, was Lord Lieutenant of the County of Durham and first Colonel of the Durham Militia. He was a noted agriculturalist and planted many of the woods around Raby as well as employing John Carr to undertake alterations to the Castle. The Earl died in 1792 and was succeeded by his only son **William Harry, 3rd Earl of Darlington** who was also a politician, and a foremost supporter of the Reform Bill of 1832. For these services, he was created **Duke of Cleveland** in 1833. An enthusiastic horseman, it was he who collected many of the sporting pictures at Raby. By his first wife, his cousin  Lady Katherine Powlett, he had three sons, and on his death in 1842 was succeeded by the eldest, known as **Duke Henry**. Like his father, the 2nd Duke was also interested in sport and politics, and took a keen interest in military matters, being Colonel of the Durham Militia from 1842-60, attaining the  rank of General in 1863. Duke Henry died in 1864 and was followed by his brother **Duke William** who died shortly after succeeding to

the title. He was followed by his brother, **Duke Harry, 4th and last Duke of Cleveland**. Before his accession he had been M.P. for Durham and later for Hastings and he continued to take an interest in politics.  He, like his brothers, had no children, and on his death in  1891, the Dukedom of Cleveland became extinct, only the Barony of Barnard remaining. Raby passed to the **9th Baron Barnard**, a descendant of Morgan, second son of Gilbert, 2nd Lord Barnard. He married Lady Catherine Cecil, daughter of the 3rd Marquess of Exeter and, on his death in 1918, was succeeded by his second son **Christopher**, the eldest son Henry having died on active service in World War I in 1917.

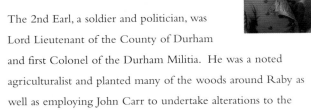

The **10th Baron Barnard** served in the Westmorland and Cumberland Yeomanry during the 1st World War and was awarded the M.C. He later commanded the 6th Battalion of the Durham Light Infantry. Lord Barnard, who was an enthusiastic sportsman, also took an active interest in the Boy Scout movement, being County Commissioner. From 1958 to 1964 he was Lord Lieutenant of the County of Durham and *custos rotulorum*. In 1920, he married Sylvia Mary (who died in 1993), daughter of Herbert Straker, M.F.H. Lord Barnard died in 1964 and was succeeded by his elder son **Harry John Neville, 11th Baron Barnard** the present owner of Raby. The 11th Baron was Lord Lieutenant of the County of Durham and *custos rotulorum* from 1970-88. During World War II, he served with the R.A.F.V.R. and in 1964 he commanded the Northumberland Hussars, and was Hon. Colonel of the 7th (Durham) Battalion the Light Infantry from 1979-89. In 1952, Lord Barnard married Lady Davina Cecil, daughter of the 6th Marquess of Exeter. In addition to the heir, Henry Francis Cecil, they have four daughters. Through his grandmother, Lord Barnard is a direct descendant of the Nevills of Raby.

The 11th and present Lord Barnard and Family in the Octagon Drawing Room by Julian Barrow, 1977.